This book is dedicated to all who are on a healing path.
I acknowledge your bravery.

May you never stop seeking support.

Illustrations by Mavgaret
Poems edited with the help of Natalie Chandra Saunders
Layout by Anna Shilonosova

ISBN 978 90 9 039315 5

Through the Vale

Poems About How Nature Brings Us Back to Life

V. Birchwood

Contents

CONTENTS

CONTENTS

The word “vale” represents many things. At the core, it means a valley. Traversing a vale can be a long and arduous journey surrounded by hills, mountains, fungus, flora, and fauna. The hike through a single vale can present a plethora of different climates, landscapes, and chapters.

A vale can also be the farewell at a funeral, the final goodbye.

“If you wish to live, you must first attend your own funeral.”
-Katherine Mansfield

As I walk one foot in front of the next, I move through the vale and bid farewell to my old self, at least the way I knew her. I welcome symbolic death to make space for rebirth. And now, as I hold myself closer than ever before, I’m supported by the nature that surrounds me, my ancestors, the friends I hold dearest, the infinite and indescribable force of love. We are all held by these profound connections.

I wrote most of these poems during the two most challenging yet healing years of my complex PTSD (c-PTSD) recovery. During this time, many sensations, feelings, memories, and emotions came up to the surface to be released. I will likely always carry pieces of them with me and I do not want to fully forget that which shaped my life — simply to have some distance and learn to love all the parts of me more tenderly.

But the publishing of this book symbolises a time where I am ready to let go (and am continuously letting go) of the impact these experiences have had on my body and mind. Writing these poems has helped to alchemise and transmute them into something different, something that can be navigated.

I intentionally chose to do so publicly, to have these parts witnessed outside of my usual container — the walls of my home, the armrests of my therapist's chair, the edges of my journals — in hopes that they might help others feel supported on their own recovery paths. I believe we are brought closer together through the art of storytelling and sharing vulnerably. After all, this practice was an innate part of the lives of our ancestors for thousands of years.

It may seem a little confusing how many different emotions appear throughout these poems. During my recovery journey, I've pendulated between bathing in the light, deep acceptance, wallowing in the darkness, and everything in between. I think this embodies the fact that healing is never linear. It happens in spirals and layers, and very often it's painful, but each time I feel that my being is even more equipped to face the next phase.

"Through the vale" is also a play on words for "through the veil." It is said, when the veil is thinnest, we are at the transitional times between life and death (spring and autumn). In these moments, there is heightened magic — creatures and spirits that guide us gently and present us with glimmers of newness, hope, and joy. In reality, these points live year-round, deep in the hollows of the forest, the echoes of a cave, the fibres of the moss, the mycelium of the fungus, the secrets of the birdsong, the rush of the river, the words of the story, the complexities of love.

The journey may be long, it may be gruelling, but the only way out is through.

A Note From the Author

As you read through these poems, I invite you to digest them not only at face value, but to remain open to their underlying ingredients. I feel that poems often need to be read a few times — marinating and fermenting — to capture the deeper intentions of the poet. You don't have to do so, of course, for I also believe that art is meant to be experienced subjectively, but I write my poems in a way that there are often multiple layers — because the world is seldom what it seems on the surface.

My belief is that we can greatly benefit from exploring art's intrinsic unapparent meanings, much as we can greatly benefit from exploring the entire world in this manner. This can serve as a means to deepen our understanding and connection with ourselves, the natural world, and most of all, each other. By examining things beyond face value, we are confronted with and supported by the magic of the world. Magic breathes all around us, but it beckons us to witness its existence.

Sapien

There is a cave on the side of the foothill.

I came upon it on a hike through the vale.

The opening snuck up on me —
a surprise out of nowhere.

I could hear the dripping, dropping
of the past rain overhead,
deep into the curves of its hollow.

I could see stalagmites, stalactites,
all those geological words,
clinging for dear life to the limestone.

I could feel the damp decay
of the mountain's innards,
the type of must that hangs on your skin.

Some would see the entrance as a chance to build a home,
but to me it felt unfamiliar, eerie, scary.

The uncertainty loomed in the coldness of its history,
the kind of chill where you can see your breath.

SAPIEN

To think they painted on these walls of stone,
depicted their lives like a story —
but if you mix enough colours you get black.

To think they built a fire on these floors laden in dust,
took a rock and bashed it against another —
but perhaps a dwelling just needs warmth.

To think they roasted meat inside on a spit,
all cuddled up, curled into each other —
but perhaps all a sapien craves is love.

Seven Days on Horseback

We must have passed
so many of them —
the bluebells, *or were they harebells?*
The hooves probably squashed a few.

I loved their delicate little petals,
so contrary to the roughness of the week.

It was only day four and I was so sore,
and I was so young,
and I felt the mare as she quivered,
the horsefly just kept biting, sucking,
and I didn't know what to do.

I didn't know what to do.
I didn't know what to do.

We'd settle in for the evening
and do our nightly things.
We'd splash our faces with the cold numb
of the river and fill our bellies
with fish from upstream.

We'd soak in the smoke of the fire,
and practice our language, get a little smarter,
forage any edible fungus *(hopefully)*,
cut potatoes in the palm of our hand *(carelessly)*,
and listen to the crickets in the tall grass field.

I'd pick the blooming chicory,
and we'd tie my horse to the trunk of the silver
birch just before going to sleep.
I'd run my fingers through her mane and
hear the whispers respond,
"*Əydə, xəyerle tön.*"[1]

For a few minutes we'd linger
with the Northern star suspended.

At that moment, this was the closest I was to
the braided women who came before me.
But back then, I could not even fathom
how near to them I'd now be.

Tatar:

[1] *Əydə,* xəyerle tön: come on (let's go), goodnight

Mordant

I was born into the vat of mordant.

It cleaved to my infant body
like oak bark tannins to flax fibres,
sticky quercitannic acid.
I was formulated for this matter chemically,
for the future, for my diegesis.

When you dipped this cloth into the
almost, but not-yet boiled water,
the kind infused with madder,
woad, weld, some other
botanical nomenclature,
I didn't feel a thing.

Except the blisters,
when they finally surfaced
like molehills
cropping up in your orchard.
My strands would absorb everything
in the remembering season.

At times, my only option was to
set my filaments alight,
brush up the pile of ash
with a birch besom broom.

MORDANT

I've learnt to set my
carefully loomed and woven
fabric in the shinelight.

To drape myself gently above
the May sweetgrass meadow
on a hemp clothesline,
slowly sunbleaching,
to expose the core of who I am.

But who am I?

My chemistry still contains the residue
of dyestuffs in the cauldron.

I will not brighten evenly,
nor consistently,
nor completely,
yet I welcome the entanglement,
fading and saturating,
contracting and expanding.

These molecules built my mass
but our bond builds someone new.

The Flood

The city dampens in an instant
and we are covered in a blanket,
but the snow will melt in a few days
and it'll all go back to noise again.

My world floods because
everything changes,
and my tear ducts leak too
and then my thawing heart.

And this moment nearly takes me
there —
to the base of the sleeping mountain,
to the height of the beeches up above,
and the transmuting silence of the night.

When I wished we could have nursed the owlet
back to health then let them go the next week.

When we could hear the flakes take their landing
on the branches and cones so effortlessly.

When we wrote all those existential things and placed
the paper under some slate until there was mush.

When we still felt the danger of being alive,
but it was just different and I didn't mind.

Everything was quieter,
and, sure, I still had problems and I got lost,
a lot,
but it was nice in a way –
at least with grief my heart opened up to love.

In a concrete jungle there is also
a whole world unfolding,
but I lose my vision some of the time
or, rather, it takes all my willpower not to.

I follow the path on the ice and continue to resist,
sometimes I slip,
and I mumble to myself,
"I don't want to become jaded or disconnected or hollow.
Unless I am the inside of the tree – then that's alright."

At least in there it is dark – charred black,
and I can't see the halogens
and the street lights glowing.

And the only fog looming in the distance
is made of crystalline droplets, not a sea of
greenhouse gases.

And the only scuttling is of the
forest creatures or the people I love,
not unpredictable factors flinging at all angles.

But I don’t want to look back or reminisce,
only to create something else for the future.

They say living in nostalgia oppresses us
and life can’t be the same as before.

But where there’s a brush, I’ll craft a new one.

I’ll illustrate every line and dip and crack
and bend and loop and fork
and crevice of this greenwood,
and one day, I’ll call it mine.

She

bathed me
not with sponges
but the softness of
her light,
and my toes were
nearly frozen.

She wrapped
them in lunar wool
and tucked them into
linen crinkled sheets
and asked each star
to kiss me.

Solstice

December 21st

This was the moment when
everything died:

The woman with the long, brown braids
spent the last five weeks
picking red and white caps
with their striking, milky gills.

Strung to magnificent ancient pines,
kept in socks over blazing yurt fires,
infused in the flaxen, tepid nectar —
drying them, preparing them,
extracting them.

Her almost-black leather boots left
footprints in the fresh coat on the ground,
crafting a trail that forked on the journey.
She roamed for more than just herself —
for an entire community.

And they revered her, listened to her,
in her crimson and snowy tunic,
as she stretched out her spine
on the mottled cream and brown fur,
watched as the smoke rose
out of the dead centre.

And then the magic brushed in
like the subtle heat
of the fresh-lit stove,
like the resilient heartwood
of the oldest tree,
like the deep iridescence
of the raven's feather.

And above the perimeter
of the tied-taut skins
she met the equal creatures —
nine of them in total with their
all-knowing, puffing bellows,
sagacious, extended antlers.
They see far more than us.

Below, still inside the shelter,
she was held closely by
Muscimol, Muscarine, Ibotenic,
Polaris, Umay Ana, Tengri,
and many others who wish to remain hidden.

The passage felt like hours,
maybe seconds,
but she made her way back home
as they took parts of her,
pulled them off like sheets of sticky honeycomb,
contained them, some type of shedding.

Exchanged for a basket filled with treasure,
not from neat, paper-packed boxes,
or from buried, concealed troves,
but wisps of light from forest orbs.

And she nurtured each in her hands
like cosmic crystal marbles,
the eyes of Earth and Sky,
Mother and Father,
Life and Death,
Spring and Autumn.

Inside, they all waited patiently
for her homecoming,
and as she arrived with her
luminescent spheres, with her
wisdom from beyond, with her
dusting of star gleam,
they were all rebirthed
on the day when the light returned.

The Beekeeper

We'd set up camp on the train for two days,
and sleep soundly as the tracks rocked our carriage
like mothers soothing babies.

A feast of railway garden cucumbers,
pastries stuffed with cabbage sold by grandmothers
in headscarves,
sunflower seed shells scattered on the red carpet,
scalding black tea from the kettle near the toilet,
a spoon of condensed milk.

The stickiness would coat my hands as I moved
down the corridor past men playing cards.
They smelled of rye beer and stale tobacco
and made remarks.

Even when we reached the smog of the city,
a place of roughnecks and a million,
the journey kept uncoiling,
so we'd follow the sound
of the buzzing.

The car with a spare diesel tank when you'd flip
a little switch dropped us off at the dirt road,
a dusty, unending path that led
to a place with many hand-built shacks,
one for every grandchild.
I got to pick my own.

Inside the attic of the furthest left,
there was a cloth-covered divan,
a safe haven for the bees to
seek refuge in winter.

When the first frost settled in,
they'd fly through an open pane,
cling their vibrating bodies
to the pilled upholstery,
and after a lingering nap,
leave from the same window
at the earliest hints of spring.

I remember the ceiling-length drums
filled with the viscous gold,
tasting of millet and
cornflowers with a note of
summer melon.

He'd turn the tap as the amber
oozed into plastic water jugs,
setting a few aside for the neighbours —
trading for oil, for squashes,
for hope.

Boldly, he'd reach his
tough hands into the hive.
I'd ask where his suit was, you know,
the funny one
with the white hat and net at the face.
"The bites are good for me," he'd smile.

We'd stand nearby and get lost in the humdrum
of the colony.
Once, a worker got caught in my hair and stung me.
I didn't know I was allergic yet.

After a long harvest day, we'd play
river games in the mud water,
not far from the grazing cows.
I'd keep my mouth shut tight
avoiding the splashes,
but it was impossible not to scream
with joy.
I was up all night vomiting.

I'd spend hours with the village girls —
two sisters the ages of seven and nine.
I'd sob as they'd bathe outside
in a filthy tin tub,
or hide from the fist of their father.
I asked about them the following year —
their lives had been met with
unimaginable tragedy.

I felt I knew the Beekeeper from your tales —
like when he tried to grow a third row of teeth
by eating only raw carrots.
Or when he brought home the wild fox and it
bit your foot, then ate all your shoes.
Or when he built the wooden airplane
and you test-flew it.
Or when you felled the tree for New Year's, hiked it
through the forest's December powder
and got horribly lost.

And he was the one you thought would live to be 113,
but when he left at 84, the whole illusion shattered.

Wrap around my scabmoss bark and throw
yourself down at my base to breathe.

Our backs are up against each other as the
beetles run in spiral motions down.
They tickle so I'll drop my cones
for the bairn to collect tomorrow
or some inquisitive witch
or a funeral offering.

I'll surrender my exhale if you bless me with your in.

My leaves bud and die in seasons,
as I rest for 300 years or more.

My branches try to take the weight of the world,
and when I can no longer, my friends will support me.

They intertwine their roots with mine,
woven in an underground network.

They feed me nutrient nectar through a line
and consult with the fungi.

And if I collapse from the highest point,
I will still be.

Love Is Not Self-Sacrifice

I do not need to jump
in front of a bullet for you,
fight on the front lines for you,
feed the last crust of bread to you.

I merely need to meet you
in your humanness,
be touched by your
desire to receive,
and my desire to give.

I feel the simmering in my heart,
and prepare these groats of buckwheat
for you,
of my own volition.

Ode to Light

In the daylight you can almost see through it —
at least the glow inside, framed
elegantly by the hand-carved blocks.

Now it's all his(s)tory —
those who worked hard,
earnestly.

It doesn't matter if it's real or fair,
but it was theirs to tell
700 years before.

And if art is the greatest act of rebellion,
for them it was the greatest act of devotion.
How carefully they cut every piece, set
each pane into a rounded frame with a point.

Though I search,
I can only somewhat see through myself.

So I make peace with sometimes
merely letting the light bounce off me,
shine through me,
disperse onto those around me,
and perhaps that is enough.

I invite you to imagine a golden light as it covers your entire being, like the warmth of a feathery blanket.

Your roots begin to dig deep into the fertile soil below and mingle with the other creatures underground.

Your branches and freshly outstretched leaves reach high into the sky above.

How does it feel to be a tree for a moment?

We Can Never Truly Know

I'll just enjoy the rain for what it is,
here now, maybe gone the next,
sometimes feeling like
it'll last for years.

And we can never truly know
the age of the tree,
the exact moment of its conception.

But it still stands out, in the valley,
when the mist rolls through
and then the night falls,
creepingly, as it always does.

And we can never truly know
the heat of the flame,
the exact moment of its ignition.

But it still burns out, in the valley,
when the mist rolls through
and then the night falls,
eerily, as it always does.

And we can never truly know
the rush of the river,
the exact moment of its formation.

But it still runs out, in the valley,
when the mist rolls through
and then the night falls,
silently, as it always does.

Kük Kükrəw

(Kük kükrəw)[1]

My spine against a tepid wooden floor
and above the flashes of *yəşen*[2].
"It finally cooled down today,"
my linen curtains say and tremble.

And I'm grateful for the
tin roof above my head
that shields me from
the rumble in the distance.

That saves me from *yañğır*[3],
and all I can muster is,
"Rəxmət Tengri, rəxmət!"[4]
I'm sobbing and I'm laughing.

(Kük kükrəw)

Tatar:
[1] *Kük kükrəw:* thunderstorm (the pronunciation sounds similar to the sound thunder makes)
[2] *yəşen:* lightning
[3] *yañğır:* rain
[4] *Rəxmət Tengri, rəxmət!:* thank you Tengri (god of the sky in Tengrism), thank you!

I feel immense grief and helpless joy,
I live in complete awe and utter dismay,
and I lean into being here.

I think of *minem ata-babalarım*[5],
I beg *yılğa*[6] to contain my tears,
I ask for *ağaç*[7] to help me breathe,
and for *qoşlar*[8] to fly with my fears.

For sometimes this world
feels far too heavy for me
to balance on my back alone,
and so I weep for their support.

(Kük kükrəw)

---

[5] *minem ata-babalarım:* my ancestors

[6] *yılğa:* the river

[7] *ağaç*: the tree

[8] *qoşlar:* the birds

First Snow

Who was I
a year ago
and who am I

Today:

When I walked
in the first snow —
dog paw flakes,
and the stone house
we never bought
and the garden
we never sowed
and the children
we never raised.

But I have the
powdered branches
and I have the
puffed up birds
and I have the
cradled embers.

And I have love,
and I know you're well.

Stigma

Sweet Spring
pressed her fragrant lips
upon the nape of my neck.

She arrived as a breeze,
concealed like stigma
on a budded branch.

She opened my
washi paper pages —
an ode to her
in haikus:

"For the heart
That doubts not,
The white flowers of the plum."
-Mokuin

STIGMA

One day, I randomly acquired a collection of Japanese haikus in a small lot of vintage books. First released in 1950, the book *Haiku (Vol. II): Spring* by R.H. Blyth made its way into my possession. Blyth shares a collection of some of the best Japanese haikus from early haiku writers, some from hundreds of years ago.

I felt inspired to read them, as a lover of poetry and themes on nature and seasons. As I was flipping through the pages, one haiku in particular caught my attention. Now and then throughout the book, some haikus are printed on washi paper overlaid on ink illustrations with haikus drawn on them by Japanese artists. A washi page between numbers 300 and 301 in the book (it doesn't even have its own page number technically) had the haiku referenced in "Stigma," printed on a translucent page over the illustration *A Torii and the Plum-Blossoms.* It became my favourite haiku in the entire book. I was quickly struck by inspiration, and the poem "Stigma" was born from what I felt after reading, *"For the heart /That doubts not, /The white flowers of the plum. /-Mokuin."*

I tried to find information on the early haikuist and illustrator Mokuin, or about this particular artwork, to no avail. It is such a beautiful piece, yet the backstory remains a mystery.

Extract from *Haiku (Vol. II): Spring* by R.H. Blyth is reprinted by kind permission of Angelico Press Ltd.

Season's Premiere

Sometimes I make snacks
and go out and watch the nature.
It moves so slowly –
no stunts, no gore
(well… actually),
no CGI, no season's premiere
(not in *that* sense),
but that's how I like it.

Almost nothing happens
but everything is happening.

The mushrooms are speaking
with the windswept trees,
the ants are going on
an adventure of a lifetime,
the birds are dancing
and trying to mate,
the dew drops are settling
on red leaves of maple –
****! I dropped some popcorn.

The Keeper of the Lost Art of Others

The protector of the
vase, candleholder, brooch, and garment,
delicately and skilfully,
playfully *(painfully)* made —
lovingly brought to fruition.

We nearly forgot them,
but they materialised before our eyes,
on the dusty shelves of the charity shop,
the vast abyss of the blackhole Internet,
the weedy corners of the backstreet
with a soggy paper sign.

And I welcomed them, embraced
them in the cushions of my palms,
"Come here, as you are," softening,
I mirror their imperfectness.

My walls are covered,
imprinted by them —
the hands that crafted,
moulded, drafted, organised,
arranged, designed, and realised.

And when I get quiet, truly still,
I hear their makers' mumbled secrets
contained by mediums and time.

Micro Doses of Grief

The rain outside made the street lamp
transform into a copper halo.
Your voice crackled
on the other end of the line.
It was midnight and you told me,
"Life is micro doses of grief."

When I grieve in the bath,
I can hardly feel the tears on my face.
They mix with my sweat and the steam and the water.
They roll down to meet their community, the pool.

When I grieve in the forest, I cry sloppy, meaty tears.
They splat on my face like they're torrential,
and I swear
the trees feel them too.

When I grieve at the river,
I cry tears that won't only be mine to carry.
They'll be contained, they'll move through and
be sent to the ocean and lake to hold.

When I grieve in the arms of my friends,
I cry tears of let-go. I'm so afraid of *this* disappearing,
but the deeper I love, the more I will lose,
so I grieve and surrender it all.

Ay!

Follow the four bends
like the curvature of bows
without arrows, inside
the flicker of usually still candles,
glowing stones, bubbling kettle.

The animal skins
tightly hung and strung
to a form with no corners,
so encompassing like *her*,
inviting, hospitable, bright
yort[1] — with a true centre.

Their camp was only
nineteen days old but
they'd scuffle and shuffle
by the fire, legs,
mostly thighs,
shaky and achey,
pointing up to her, exclaiming,

"Ay!"[2]

Tatar:

[1] *yort*: house, yurt

[2] *ay*: moon, also month

But she did not move
and neither the stars —
maybe slowly, surely
creepingly nomadic,
as they were busy sleeping
but not before their eyes.

She'd be unfazed yet
change in phases,
Ural tawları[3] would tell
stories millenniums old,
and the mare up the hill
would let out a heavy sigh.

[3] *Ural tawları*: the Ural mountains

Justice

You walked up to the intercom
as we stood on the road at the edge of the fence.
I am one drop in the spring of those who love you.

You pressed the little button and
a woman's voice appeared on the speaker,
"Halló?"
"Hello? I need to come in. My name is N."
"OK, just enter through the gate but you have to come alone."

How could this be happening to you?
The person who will not kill a fly,
who picks up abandoned trash,
who drinks cacao on my sofa,
who fights for the marginalised,
who embraces me and gives so vulnerably.

I felt the starkness of your reality
as we observed the barren landscape:
no trees, no telephone lines, no sunshine.
If *I* was feeling this way,
then how was it for *you?*

You moved through to the inside.
That was the last time I saw you for a month.

After your release,
I picked you up from the halfway house.
You had a curfew at 22:00,
so we went and got sushi
and drove by the sea
and talked about violence against women
and at exactly 21:45,
I left you at the unassuming door.
We were always 15 minutes early,
just in case.

You told me about your time in prison,
how you made friends with the other inmates,
how you cooked dinner for them
or played counsellor,
how you made art,
ink and watercolour drawings on thick paper.
"The room was pretty nice,"
you joked.

They classed you as a "violent criminal"
but it was rare to find a soul as soft,
as gentle as yours.

I remember the first day we met —
we ended up at the Japanese cake house
in the harbour district.
The red-blue ships stood massive in the biting water,
and we ordered a rice bowl and a pot of tea to share.

I excused myself to the bathroom
and carefully washed my arctic-kissed hands.
I felt the overflowing of my heart.

I already knew I loved you.

You told me about the night it all happened,
still imprinted fresh on your body,
protecting yourself from years of enduring,
harmed by the one meant to keep you safe.

They were all meant to keep you safe.

Years later and our connection only deepened.
How do you even define the type of
love that transcends any label prescribed,
that neglects to express what we really are?

Sometimes justice is not served, in fact, it often isn't.
But I hold hope a day will come when it can be.

Until then I'll hold you and all who share your story
and we'll carry this weight for the whole of humanity.
Because the world says love heals all
and how could I do anything but love you?

I Am Here

My frail body is alive
and I've put parts of me
on hold to love the ones that
find this all too much,
and not enough,
and more than I could ask for.

To love the ones
whose ankles sting from nettle,
who walk on sunken soles,
whose toes try not to crumble,
fumble inwards.

To love the ones
whose hearts could not swell any further,
who feel like an endless streaming fountain,
who question what will life be like in a year.

And I left the baubles hanging long past the dead winter.
And that which I long for must be explored another time.

Mother Moon

When I was younger and
I felt the emptiness,
I'd look up to her,
radiant in her stillness.

Trusting in her sphere
that wouldn't 180 when it
had enough, so I could
be lit by her love.

The holes in the ground
could've been mistaken
for a bear's den.
You could hibernate in there
all winter long and wake up
in the spring to birdsong,
to clay pots of yellow ochre,
sunbathing all powdery at the cliff edge.

If we could view the scene as a projection,
our perception would be prehistoric,
as they dug up the dust,
scutching and hackling,
spinning the stinging nettles
into lanky fibres,
warp and weft on a loom,
finished by the ferric mustard dye.

I invite you to imagine the nameless individuals who came before you, who formed the reality of your present existence, who carry so much love for you.

Does a scene come to mind?

Where are your ancestors located?

What are they doing?

Do they have a message to share with you?

Íslenskt Sumar

On winter mornings like these
I long for *íslenskt sumar*[1]
and my muddy piggies in the hot pool.

It's still only eight degrees
but I have never felt this type of warmth
or joy inside my wilderness heart.
I'm held by the *brönugras*[2] sun that started to set
but changed his mind, only to rise,
and come back to me once more.

And he'll pose on cotton candy clouds,
spread out like some ancient god
begging to be carved out of stone.
He'll even brush the nape of *Esja mín*[3],
who conceals herself with the faintest
remnants of last April's *snjór*[4].

Icelandic:

1 *íslenskt sumar*: Icelandic summer

2 *brönugras*: heath spotted orchid (*Dactylorhiza maculata*)

3 *Esja mín*: my Esja, the mountain that overlooks Reykjavík city

4 *snjór*: one of the many Icelandic words for snow

And I'll wiggle my feet and inhale
the hanging of *harðfiskur*[5] on the beach,
the mash of seaweed floating in the water,
the rot of the little shack with the birch roof,
or the sound of *kría*[6] guarding nests mercilessly
(please don't dive bomb me).

And there is a choir singing in the distance.
And there is no hint of night for two more months.

---

[5] *harðfiskur*: dried fish, a popular snack of dried cod fish

[6] *kría*: Arctic tern, a very territorial bird that a lot of people are fearful of that is frequently found in Iceland

What the Glow Worms Said

When we were lost,
in complete darkness,
I surrendered to the spruce grove
and bumps on flesh, formed
by the path down to the river.

The canopy so thick,
it concealed the Great Bear,
nothing to be seen but
the wriggling wee things
plopped there on the Earth,
our unexpected guides.

The mesmerising bioluminescent specks
appeared, and said, *"keep going."*

We tracked them,
and the sound of the gushing,
startled by the cracking
twigs behind the bushes,
and a face full of spider webs,
until we reached her, and paused.

During our expedition, a clearing came,
an entire valley illuminated,
not a single cloud in sight –
but certainly a world full of stars.

I could barely see your body,
but I could hear your voice.

So we jumped in freezing water,
we screamed piercingly,
we cut our soles on rocks,
we laughed hysterically,
we mooned the moon,
and we followed the glow worms home.

Kiyez İteklər

The turquoise of the housefront
with the pine logs neatly stacked,
framed you at the door and
I thought to myself,
"You're beaming!"

There was a line of fresh tracks.

You lived on the other side of the village,
the faraway part –
but when we were both there,
it didn't matter the distance
or how cold, even -30 degrees.

We'd slip our feet into *kiyez iteklər*[1]
and try not to slip on the ice at the walkway.
I imagined *əbi*[2] bartered
for mine with the neighbour
and *əniyeñ*[3] found a maker in the city.

Tatar:

1 *kiyez iteklər*: felted wool winter boots

2 *əbi*: grandmother

3 *əniyeñ*: your mother

A jute rope attached to a sled
was wrapped around your hand
and the snow grew attached
to the wool of our boots,
and I grew attached to you.

Our minds just worked the same,
as we'd fly down the hill until sunset.
We'd lay out in the powdered garden,
staring up to the sky.
We could have been out there for days.

But now, neither of us can return,
yet these are the moments we carry,
wrapped in hemp cloth,
tucked away in a bast basket,
stuck to our brains like frost
to the lanolin of our *kiyez iteklər*.

Except no matter how much we cry
and fight and scream and plead,
they will not let us felt a new pair.

Green Sun

Don't we all live like this?

With muted smells,
muted colours,
muted tastes.

With feeling like the
room is closing in
and brain shakes
settled by adrenaline.

Don't we all leave our
bodies when they've
had too much?
But most things are.

It's like the green sun —
an underlying display of truth,
when what the atmosphere projects
is a completely different hue.

I saw the world for what it was
when the filter was removed.
No more a faded, foggy haze
but now a vivid, vernal view.

The Elevator Back From Therapy

First
it starts with the bathroom check:

The salt ions running down my cheeks,
a little pat of toilet paper folded into a square,
the dried-up rings like faery circles
in the forest under my eyes,
and there's so much snot –
I suck it back,
I nearly feel it hit my brain.

I walk down the corridor and press
the downwards arrow,
I spiral, I'm spiralling.

The polished doors pull away from each other,
a parting of the seas.
There's a mirror inside
and all I see is me.

Obsidian Butte

Your stack of black rocks in the corner
are glossy and smooth to the touch,
and when I hold them up to the grubby sun,
they're see-through.
You gifted me a river-rolled one.
It's protected by an Art Deco box on
my mantelpiece.

"There's a spot called Obsidian Butte,"
you told me,
"That's where I found this slab."
So Sunday we traded our sand for that one
and we drove to the hills.
We could see the jet masses huddled up
on the horizon.

And as we hiked, got closer,
there they were — sheltering by the
water of the toxic lake
(not the type for bathing).
They weren't so different from us,
hiding from the midday glare,
by the bunkers or the water tanks.

The next week you strolled up to me,
"Let's all drive to Joshua Tree,"
so we packed up
our bags full of shiny rocks,
and climbing gear,
and food in tin cans,
and again we traded our sand for another,
(or is all this sand one sea of the same?)

We knew we had arrived when the
first of many stood out in the distance,
like a scene from a children's book
with quirky, angular branches, crowned
by palm tufts like porcupines.
The basin hadn't met rain for months.
The jackrabbits scavenged in the manzanitas.

We made friends quickly, the dirtbags,
(don't worry, it's an affectionate term).
We projected movies on boulder sides
and made Dutch oven roasts buried in embers,
told lantern-lit stories about our lives,
knocked on van windows for conversation,
and got licked awake by the coyotes.

One evening, when the campfire raged
and we could see the Milky Way,
we were offered an invitation, initiation.
Fifteen of us gathered, tromping
through the desert until
we reached the unassuming rock.
The spiny beings were shadows in the dark.

All of us lined up single file,
as we traversed the stone,
not a flashlight in sight,
pitch like the obsidian,
following the experienced ones,
the sound of their voices,
or maybe our own intuitions.

I felt the breeze from outside
as I slid through the first and last canal.
Somehow, after far too many contractions,
we were birthed from the chasm
in the middle of the night.
We stood above the vast wilderness,
the Sublime,
and we laughed beneath the celestial souls.

Four years later there were flash floods and fires,
and by then we all went our own ways.
L. passed in the twisted metal,
A. was consumed by a real demon,
M. left his body when it could sustain him no more.

But you? You're somewhere out there,
and I hope the world is gentle on you.
I can't forget how tenderly you cared for me,
when I was at rock bottom in my life.

I Can Almost See Jan Mayen From Here

If I strain my eyes
and look far enough
out into the Greenland sea
and ignore the fisherman
pulling the sisal rope
at the harbour docks
and imagine my feet
leaving the black sand,
the lava rock
of Sheepriverhook,
and swim for a while
avoiding polar bears
somehow keeping warm,
I'll hit the island's shore.

Moulting

Frigid to the touch
my scales pop out
as I moult my old skin.

It shrivels down the length
of a metre,
vertabra by vertabra,
and god it takes forever to
get the bloody thing
off of me.

But once it hits the end,
the tip of my tail,
I wait for it to get gritty,
roll around in the desert dirt,
shrivel in the heat of the sun.

I embrace my new appearance,
a layer underneath once hidden,
and when I look out
I see a mirage on the horizon —
the rustly old date palm, the oasis
concealed beyond a minefield.

The cast remains close to me
but over time it decomposes,
back to the earth
and I am drinking from clear water.

To Me, You Are Many Things

I could trace the remnants of your
footprints in the fresh coat on the ground,
as you walked down in the valley,
as you stared up to the moon —
the rosy hint of frost and alpenglow,
the silhouettes of cedars, larches, pines.
The same beauty I'm entranced by,
basking in the stillness, silence,
bloom.

And to me, you are many things:

The lantern that gently sways,
amongst a sea of white flakes,
that swings from the cottage wall
witnessing the passers-by,
taking it all in with a
resplendent, thawing glow.

The river that slowly rushes
and explores and branches
and threads through every
part of this world, that binds it
all naturally, interconnected
simply through its being.

The whisper of a shadow
with its back against a tree
and it looks up, to revel in
the wisdom of old growth,
leaves that oscillate,
refulgent like rain.

The Milky Way I-am-so-fond-of,
a complexity of stars, still alive,
all scattered in the most
artful and present way,
steadfast even when not seen,
full of so much more to learn from.

The flame of the taper with
its contained, intrinsic warmth,
by proximity each fibre sets alight
when close to another wick, breathing
life into others, losing naught,
transmuted from a fire never dimming.

And I don't know by what magic
we were both brought to this Earth,
kindred spirits, sentient souls,
at the same speck of time,
gifted with the chance
to grow together and separate.

And I do think of you often.
And I do care for you deeply.
And I do love you boundlessly.

(Thank you, for being my friend).

In the house down by the creek,
the morning hearth embers and keeps,
and all my feelings cover over,
like the vernal valley's clover.

The river's run contains my grief,
and in death's wintering I sleep,
for all the prior seasons passed,
each held a place in timing's cast.

The languid stillness of the moon,
each star entangled and attuned,
right when I least expected change,
though it on nature's tether hangs,

My layered heart opened to you,
like the spring's magnolia bloom.

I invite you to imagine a place in this world where you feel the safest.

Are you inside or outside?

What is the weather like?

How does the space smell?

What elements do you see around you?

What can you hear?

Are there any visitors?

Ancient Beings

The trees rustle their leaves
just before the storm rolls in.
This is their first warning —
and then the subtle weight in the air
and the daylight falls
and the terrain is transformed
once more — it never stays the same.

My ancestors knew how to read
the ancient beings,
how to truly see and hear them,
how to learn from the
nightingale who quickly shelters
or the moss that absorbs until engulfed,
uncertain but trusting of the next drink.

And when I open myself up to truly listen,
I carry the wisdom of indigeneity in my body.

I Hope This Is the Last Hot Day of Summer

In late August, all you can do is
beg for the breeze,
and maybe a gust will be kind
and push you over
the edge.

Or maybe you are the giant sequoia,
who knows how to take the heat.

(But what if you don't want to?)

Sometimes it's there, just sweltering
all around,
magnified by every thing:

Bay window, perfume bottle,
crystal inkwell, tincture vial,
water carafe, looking glass.

You're left in the jar to ferment,
or grieve on the stone floor.

Everything in Its Place

I wanted the nice home to call my own —
everything in its place.

Every drawer organised, kitchen orderly,
every item its own purpose —
protection from the chaos.

But I grew up and realised the fantasy,
as reality was staring directly at me,
and this terrified me
and brought me so much suffering.

And so I learned to embody it,
embrace all the parts of me,
that beauty can happen amidst the
complete disorder of things.

Countervortex

When I look out beyond what's in my hands, I can experience:

The light as it seeps through the brassy leaves of the copper beech,
for a moment I feel transcendent.

The curvaceous shadow of my standing lamp against the wall,
I can sense its form shrouded in mystery.

The morning sun as it floods through my wall-length windows,
and it will shift before my eyes again.

The batting clouds that kiss the roofs of my neighbours,
and they feel frozen in time.

I pendulate between these and my:

Deepest grief — the floor-dropping kind,
where I'm face first in my own bodily fluid puddle.

Pure anguish — the stomach-wrenching type,
where I can hardly move an inch with these knots.

Immense shame — that seems filthy and dirty
and I feel I cannot wash it off of me.

Desperate despair — that clings to my bones and reappears
like cobwebs in the corner of the basement.

Bitter jealousy — that makes me crawl out of my skin, into my shell,
and I never want to see the world again.

COUNTERVORTEX

This vortex sucks me down and I'm whirlpooling so fast,
I don't know how to paddle my way back up without simply
drowning.

Sometimes, I attempt to float on my back.
Sometimes, I surrender and just let it happen.

And sometimes, when I'm underwater,
just about to forfeit the last of my air, a light appears,
like they say you'll see at the end, except I'm still very much alive.

It's here — the countervortex,
the upwards energy spiralling soon makes me resurface,
I gasp for oxygen, relieved to breathe again.

The two vortexes live, amalgamating inside of me,
like some cosmic, alchemical dance.
My clever body knows homeostasis, how to find its own way,
I am merely a facilitator, the outside world merely a supporter.

Suddenly that which once tried to suck me down
doesn't need to disappear,
because there's enough inside to suspend me there, buoyant.

The basin of this lake can carry all the beauty and hopelessness.

And so much of the beauty that I witness in the world
is the presence living in others,
yet so much of the beauty I experience in the world
is the presence living in me.

This poem is inspired by techniques taught in Somatic Experiencing.

Ode to River

In the swelling of the summer
when there's just been a downpour,
she rushes murky grey
like the puddles at the edge of my
grandmother's village.

I can see the cumulonimbus
lurking in the distance
and although they look angry,
I'm comforted by them.

Now, at least for a little while,
we can stop chopping wood
and carrying water,
two buckets at a time.

The air starts to relieve its pressure,
resigning from its perch on our shoulders.

I'll pass the little chapel
and the only convenience store for hours,
(how inconvenient).

I'll wander down the trail
to find respite at her banks.

I was there just as I am now,
though back then
I wish I had the words to say,
"Sez monda minem beløn."[1]

Tatar:
[1] *Sez monda minem beløn:* You (all) are here with me

Skototropism

I don't have the words to express
all the ways you shaped me
as I reached towards the
nutrient-rich darkness,
as the microbes grasped
around my waking tendrils.

Leaning into the shadows unearthed
the depth at which
I deserve to be loved,
and so do you.

The deeper into the abyss I expanded,
the closer I flourished towards the light.

You witnessed my chlorophyllic organelles
as they sustained this evolution.

And now that I have absorbed the sun-warmth,
imprinted on my epidermis,
I cannot go back.

And now that I have felt a tree trunk's bark,
gently guiding my shoots,
I cannot go back.

And now that I have heard the crying of the macaws,
signalling it's time,
I cannot go back.

Emerging into the illuminated,
I cannot unlearn what was revealed
whilst grounding in the void.

Acknowledgements

Thank you to the brilliant people who beta read my poems before they were published and provided feedback: Ana Filipa Piedade; Ann Oh; Blue Jay Walker; Kaïra Luna Innaro; Katja Saupe; Laura A. Wolf; Lucia U.; Madison Bouse; Matias Bünger; Olivia Ash, Esq., MS.

Thank you to Aygul Ahmetcan for proofreading the Tatar.

Thank you to Magnús Þór Einarsson for proofreading the Icelandic.

A special thank you to Alex, Bee, Jack, Jhamil, Maggi, Mirte, Monique, my father, Nara, Natalie, Paul, R., Rohan, S., Xav, and my other beautiful friends that I am so deeply honoured to be loved by, who supported and encouraged this dream and helped to make it a reality. You are all truly my chosen family.

About the Author

Vasi Birchwood (she/her) is an Indigenous (Volga Tatar) poet, filmmaker, colourist, hand sewer, singer, and storyteller. She has an MA in Creative Writing and this is her first poetry book. On her YouTube channel, she covers historical fashion and experimental archaeology, including the deeply meaningful reconstruction and research of her Indigenous clothing, as well as conscious consumption, our innate connection to nature, and the wisdom we each carry from our ancestors.

Made in the USA
Las Vegas, NV
26 December 2024

15380856R00055